The

Investeenager

All rights reserved; no part of this publication may be reproduced, stored in a retrieval system, or transmitted in any form or by any means - electronic, mechanical, photocopy, recording, scanning, or otherwise except for brief quotations in critical reviews or articles, without the prior written permission of the Publisher. This book may not be lent, resold, hired out, or otherwise disposed of by way of trade in any form of binding or cover other than that in which it is published without the Publisher's prior written consent.

While every effort has been made to ensure that the information in this book is accurate, no liability can be accepted for any loss incurred in any way whatsoever by any person relying solely on the information contained herein. No responsibility for loss occasioned to any person or corporate body acting or refraining from acting due to reading the material in this book can be accepted by the author or his company.

Table of Content

Acknowledgments 5

Prologue 7

Chapter 1 What Is Investing? 11
    Banking is Not Saving! 12
    Inflation is Real 13
    Pay for College 13
    Play the Long Game 15

  Why Invest at Your Age? 16

  What Does Investing Mean? 18

  What is a Stock? 20

Chapter 2 Types of Stock Investing 23
  Mutual Funds 23

  Index Funds 25

  Exchange Traded Funds (ETFs) 26

  Single-Stock Investing 27

Chapter 3 Investment Terms Simplified 31
  Volume 31

  Market Capitalization 32

  High and Low 33

  Price-to-Earnings Ratio 34

  Open & Close 35

Chapter 4 Starting Your Investing Journey 37
  Making Money To Invest 37

Neighborhood Jobs *38*
Household Chores *39*
Sell Old Items *39*

How Much Money Should You Invest? 43

Chapter 5 What To Look For In A Stock? 47

The Company's History 47

The Company's Plans 49

The Charts 50

Chapter 6 Best Investing Platforms For Beginners 57

Robinhood 58

Webull 59

Chapter 7 The Mental Game 61

Do Not Fear 61

Do Not Be Greedy 63

Listen to the Right People 63

Conclusion 67

Four Steps: 69

Acknowledgments

I want to acknowledge my mother for giving me the idea to write this book in 2020.

I also want to acknowledge my dad for pushing me to improve and always supporting me.

To my sister Shayo, thanks for helping me out with this book in a big way and being a best friend.

Finally, to my mentor and longtime friend, Kyle Dendy, thank you for helping me through the whole writing process and always giving me advice.

Prologue

Why did I write this book? I wrote this book to help teenagers interested in investing but need help knowing where to begin. I wrote this book so that, unlike me, you won't have to search for many videos, read many books, and look at dozens of articles to understand the basics.

My ultimate goal is to help teenagers understand stock investing without looking at many sources. With this book, you can become a future-thinking teenager who has prepared for anything tomorrow might hold. I will know that I succeeded with this book if I get at least one teen saying this helped them.

What credibility do I have to be teaching you anything? Well, I have been actively investing and learning about investing for over three years. Every month my dad puts money into his long term investment account, and

I manage it. I have made my mother over $1400 dollars in less then six months with just $700.

Who am I? I'm sure most of you are asking that question because I am a teenager about to teach you about investing in stocks. My name is Tosin Osowo. I am sixteen years old at the time of writing this book. I was born in Rochester, New York but raised in Dallas, Texas, where I live with my mom, dad, and sister. My father is a doctor, and my mother is a professional artist. I enjoy playing soccer, and basketball, reading, watching movies, playing video games, hanging out with friends, and investing.

Now, before we get going, I must clarify one thing. You can only invest in the stock market once you are at least eighteen years old. Wait! Before you close the book for false advertising, let me explain why that rule does not matter.

If you are under eighteen and want to invest, all you have to do is have your parents open up an account under their name but use money from your bank account. The other option is having your parents open up a custodial account, a custodial account is just an account that you and your parents manage but it's under your name. So when you turn eighteen you take it over completely. And you would be able to use your bank account for this. The platform I recommend for a custodial account is Charles Schwab. The platforms I recommend later on are for the first option I mentioned. Since that is cleared up, let's begin!

Chapter 1

What Is Investing?

Do you like money? Assuming your response is yes (as it is for me), investing is an excellent method for generating income and amassing wealth. It is a great way to earn money without experiencing much stress.

Throughout this chapter, I will cover various reasons you should invest, especially between the ages of thirteen and eighteen. Investing is not only good, but it is also better than putting your money into any other thing.

Let's look at reason number one.

Banking is Not Saving!

When you have money saved in a bank, what usually happens to it? Nothing! In fact, your money almost loses value because most banks have low-interest rates.

(Bank Interest definition: Bank interest is the interest you get for the money you have in that account and the type of account it is). For example, let's say you put five hundred dollars into a bank for one year, and that bank had a 0.67% interest rate. At the end of that year, the five hundred dollars would be five hundred and seven dollars. Imagine working all year for seven dollars! That is hardly profitable. At the end of the year, the seven dollars' worth might not even be as much as it was at the beginning of the year.

Now, I'm not saying that you shouldn't save your money. It is wise and practical to save. I am saying that you should take some of the money you would save and invest it in stocks. Saving all your money makes sense in the short term. In the long run, you are losing out when all you do is save your money in the bank.

If you do stock investing correctly, it can lead to long-term growth for your money faster than any bank interest rate could give you.

Inflation is Real

Inflation is another reason you should invest some of your money. Inflation causes your money in the bank to decrease in value. This decrease typically happens when there is a recession in the economy.

Even if the recession is not much, inflation can still have a negative effect on your money. If you have money invested in stocks, you know your money will go up throughout the years. As the value of money decreases, you continue to make more money to help you cope with the recession. So, you don't have to be worried about inflation.

Pay for College

"About 1 in 5 Americans hold student loans. More than half of those 45 million people with federal student loans have $20,000 or less to pay, with about a third of all borrowers owing less than $10,000. Seven percent of people with federal debt owe more than $100,000" (washingtonpost.com).

Another reason you should invest, especially as a teenager, is that it can help you pay for college. Some colleges are expensive. Maybe, your parents will pay for some of it or even all of it, but you never know. Even when they pay for all of it, you can enjoy your college years better if you have a source of income separate from what your parents or guardian provides.

If you invest as a teenager, especially around 13 or 14, you could have a decent amount of money for college. You might not eventually use it, but it is good to have that safety blanket. If you consistently work on your investments, you'd be surprised how much you'll have.

Investing as a teenager plays a vital role in this plan. If you finish college with debt, big or small, as many people do, you might spend years trying to pay it off. But if you had invested since you were a teenager and through four years of college, you would save yourself a lot of trouble and enjoy every year of your college studies.

You'll be financially literate and well-educated, especially compared to your peers. Let me tell you a little secret, whenever you talk about investing to an adult, especially when you know what you are talking about, they are impressed beyond belief. It's fun watching their faces.

Being financially literate and savvy could also help you get into college. For instance, if you are interested in business, you give yourself a big edge on your college essay by knowing more than your peers about investing.

Play the Long Game

My final reason is long-term growth. It is powerful when you are young. When you look at the math, it is exciting to see how much money you can make if you invest in stocks early as a teenager or young adult.

For example, if you invest two hundred dollars every month at an eight percent yearly return, you would have one million dollars in forty-five years. Sounds awesome, right? And that is just one example of the power of long-term stock investing.

If you put in more over the year and continue to build your portfolio, you stand a chance to become a millionaire without doing even the tiniest bit of work for it. You only have to put in the funds, others do the job, and you enjoy the profits.

Why Invest at Your Age?

Why should you think about investing now? Isn't that an old-person thing? Despite picking up this book, you're probably wondering why you should start thinking about money and investing at your age when everything is still provided for you.

That is what I thought until I learned how much money you can make if you start young. What inspired me to invest at such a young age in the first place?

Many things contributed to my love for investments, including one of my favorite shows, *Shark Tank*. People from across the country present their idea, company, or product to a panel of well-established investors (sharks) looking for them to invest money to help the entrepreneur make their idea successful.

I loved the aspect of the show where the sharks (investors) decided whether a product or startup company would be a smart investment. However, my favorite thing about the show, which inspired me to learn about investing, was how these investors, Kevin O'Leary, Mark Cuban, and Lori Greiner make money while they sleep from the thousands of investments they have made over the years.

I was fascinated by how they don't have to work another day because they are making continuous passive income (passive income: making money doing no actual work or physical labor).

Something else that inspired me to invest was YouTubers such as Biaheza, Graham Stephen, and Mark Tilbury. Biaheza's channel showed me that you could be a teenager and set yourself up to have a great deal of money when you are older from investing.

Graham Stephen taught me how you could make money with the unpredictable ups and downs of the economy and market. Mark Tilbury's videos explained complex investing concepts and terminology understandably.

My closest inspiration was Ayo Osowo, my father. He is a full-time doctor who invests on the side and has made great profits. He has also lost money in other investments. But in that process, he taught me why certain investments failed so I won't make the same mistakes. He also taught me what works in investment.

He always talked about how he loved passive income because he did not have to work for that money. So, I figured if I invested at a young age, I could only imagine how much money I would have waiting for me when I was my dad's age.

Just like I realized, I hope you now understand why it is essential to start investing now. You might only make a lot of money from it all at once. But you will be grateful for it in a few years.

What Does Investing Mean?

Around the age of 14, I wanted to learn about investing. It wasn't easy because I did not have a single resource explaining the basics of investing or answering most teenagers' questions. I had to read different books, watch videos, google various terms, etc. That is why I decided to write this book. Someone my age could read it and have enough knowledge to start investing safely.

I will give you more reasons why you should invest now instead of waiting till you're 30 in the next chapter. The percentage of teenagers who invest now is about 20% which is not bad but could and should be higher. More teenagers need to start taking control of their lives before it is too late and they get into the rat race of life.

Investing is simply taking your money and applying it to an asset with the belief that it will benefit you financially or otherwise. An investment can take many forms, most notably, investing in a company, investing in real estate, investing for retirement, and investing in a stock.

The main kind of investment that I will focus on is stock investing. You can think about stock investing as a futuristic term. It means putting money into a stock with the hope of a return in profits later. Or, to be more specific, you would hold the stock you bought and not sell it for a long time until it is at a price higher than what you bought it at and sell it for that profit.

It is simple, just like any other trade you might have ever done before. Remember buying that snack from a price and holding on to it till it finished at the market. Then, your classmates came to you wanting to buy it now, and the price has increased. Yes, stock investing is something just like that! But not with snacks; you will be trading stocks.

What is a Stock?

That question is asked by millions of people every year who hear about stocks but don't quite understand what it is. Understanding what a stock is and what it is not is basic knowledge in your journey into stock investments.

A stock is part ownership of a company divided by its shares. You buy these shares, giving you fractional ownership of that company. So when you buy shares of a company, you own part of the company. That means when it is doing well or when it is doing poorly, your money is also affected in the form of your shares.

The idea in stock investing is to look for a promising company and buy its shares when its value has yet to skyrocket. Then you can sell it when the value is higher or hold on to it. Imagine you had bought a share of Apple when it first started. Your shares will be worth so much more right now. Exciting, right?

Now you should have at least a little interest in investing. Learning about stock investing at a young age and practicing it can deeply brighten your financial future.

Chapter 2

Types of Stock Investing

Now, you understand what stock investing is. Let's get into the technicalities. Don't worry! It will continue to remain fun.

This chapter will explore the most common and popular forms of stock investing, including mutual funds, index funds, ETFs, and regular stocks. These will help you decide what long-term investment you want to try out. This knowledge will give you an edge that most of your peers don't have.

Mutual Funds

The first clue to understanding mutual funds is in the word mutual. Mutual, in this context, refers to the other investors investing money in a shared investment. It is different people coming together to create a fund (known as a mutual fund). You buy shares in a mutual fund and it is managed by a professional money manager.

Think of a mutual fund as a pot of soup where thousands of investors add ingredients that would be money to be a part of various investments, including stocks and bonds. Then, it's all mixed and divided among the investors. The cool thing about mutual funds is the variety of sectors from which to choose.

One of the advantages of mutual funds is that they are professionally managed. There is also high liquidity (meaning the person running the mutual fund can buy or sell a stock/bond without the value of the mutual fund drastically changing). The diversification of the mutual fund reduces the risk of your investment.

However, you do not have a say in the mutual fund because it is controlled by a professional. It is also more expensive than ETFs or index funds, and they are not traded on the stock market.

As a teenager, mutual funds might not be the best investment for you. It is mostly because of how expensive they can be and the lack of control over what goes into a mutual fund.

Index Funds

Next, let's examine the widely popular stock investments known as index funds. Do you remember all those classes on indexes in school? Well, I hope you were paying attention in class.

When you hear the term index fund, think of it as an overall market average. Your money is invested in a variety of stocks in a specific category, and you receive interest based on the average of all holdings. One of the well-known index funds is the S&P 500, which averages the market's overall stock gains and losses. It comprises the five hundred largest U.S. companies.

One of the biggest advantages of this type of fund is the massive diversification. For example, the S&P 500 index holds the top 500 companies on the stock market, so if one stock goes down for a year, many others are probably going up. Another advantage is the limited risk. Since there is so much natural diversity in index funds, the possibility of losing money in the long term is slim.

However, the main disadvantage is that the growth of index funds can be slow even for a year. So, for teenagers, investing in an index fund is smart for the long-term growth of your money at an average rate. It might only bring in a little money at a time, but it is a secure way to build wealth for the future.

Exchange Traded Funds (ETFs)

ETF stands for Exchange Traded Fund. ETFs are similar to mutual funds. Like a mutual fund, ETFs get money from many investors and invest in several sectors. But they are unique in that they are bought and sold like stocks.

With ETFs, there are various types to choose from with distinct purposes. For example, some have bonds and stocks—other ETFs track a sector of the market like technology or health care.

ETFs are a good investment for beginners because you will typically get diversification and slow but steady growth of your money. The advantages of ETFs are that they typically cost less than a mutual fund, have a good amount of diversification, and are easier to trade.

However, the main disadvantage is tracking. For example, if you pick an ETF in the real estate sector, you must be tuned in to that world to know how your ETF will do and the right time to sell. You will also have to check how that sector's market is constantly doing. It can be challenging, so be mindful there.

While it can be a painstaking job, it can also be a good investment for teenagers. You will get to learn about different kinds of sectors with this type of investment. The affordability also allows you to decide on the sectors for your investment.

Single-Stock Investing

Now, let's talk about single-stock investing. You have probably heard more about this kind of stock investing. Regular stock investing is widely common among investors, especially beginners. You can choose the company you want to invest in and the kind of securities you want to buy with this kind of investment.

It's exciting looking at all the companies you know and love and being able to own a part of them. However, single-stock investing is riskier because your money is in one place, unlike an index or mutual fund. If the company does badly, you lose money; when it does well, you gain money.

But many companies have their stock growing consistently, like Microsoft or Apple. You want to invest in those kinds of companies. So overall, it's good to invest in single stocks.

If you diversify and invest in more than one, you don't lose all of your money if one of your stocks is falling. However, always ensure you have done extensive research on the company and looked at its stock's past and the company's plans for the future.

A major advantage is that there are numerous companies from which to choose. You don't need a lot of stocks to have great long-term growth. You'll be in good shape if you pick two or three companies with amazing long-term trajectories. Plus, it's cool to say, "I own part of Apple."

Now, the disadvantages come from the same things as the advantages. Let me explain. When buying single stocks, you generally want to diversify, so you do not put all your eggs in one basket or stock. If you have all of your money in one stock and it goes down, you have lost everything, but if you have more than one stock in your portfolio, you will be okay if one goes down because you have your money in others.

However, single stocks can be dangerous because you put your faith in that company to do well over time. Single-stock investment is a great way for teens to invest. But, it would be best if you researched your desired companies properly. If they go up, you will be happy with the money you make.

I invest in index funds and single stocks. I do index funds because while they do grow slowly, they do grow. The risk with this type of investment is little to nothing. My thought process is that when I am 30 years old, I'll have a good amount of money waiting for me since I invested in the S&P 500 consistently at 17.

If you add to it over time, you'll have a chance at even more money. I also do single stocks because if I do good research on a company, I can make money when they blow up or get bigger than they are over time.

Chapter 3

Investment Terms Simplified

In this chapter, the goal is to understand investing terminologies. You will encounter these terms when looking at a stock's statistics which can be found online or on your investment platforms.

However, explaining all the terms used in investment is practically impossible. But I can explain some of the terms used in investment, so you're not completely lost when you make your first investment move. I will cover volume, market cap, high and low, and open and close.

Volume

Starting with volume, the meaning of this term is simple. When you see volume by a stock and a number by this stock, know that number is how long that stock has been traded during that period. So, that large number by stock is the volume.

It is how many times a stock has been bought and sold during that period. One little tip when researching a stock is that you want to see a number on the larger side for volume because that means many prefer a stock because it shows people are interested in it.

Volume is important. It tells you that people are actively trading in the stock, investing in it, and how many people are interested in that company which can be a factor in whether you invest in the stock. When I see a company with high volume, I think it's probably a good investment because many people are putting their money into it, so I will make money if I buy it now.

Market Capitalization

Market Capitalization, better known as market cap, is essentially the worth or value of a company's stock. To find the market cap of a company's stock, multiply the price of a stock by how many shares a company has.

Often, investors will look at this figure to decide whether they want to invest in a company's stock.

Market cap is significant because it shows what people think of the company. The bigger the company's value, the more people want to invest. The more people invest in that company, the more money that company makes, and the more money that company makes, the more money you make.

Say there is a company called Lard & Laptops, and they have a low market cap, which is an indicator to me that I should either not invest in them because they have a low value or I should invest in them now while they are low because in some cases, low cap stocks have potential to grow. As I always say, do your research before making an investment decision. Remember to check the market cap when looking at stocks to invest in.

High and Low

Whenever you see the high number by a stock's statistics, know that it was the highest price it was bought and sold during that day. The low is the lowest price that stock traded (bought and sold) that day.

The high and low are the most important to pay attention to if you are day trading because it gives you a general sense of the stock's current worth in the market. If the low of a stock keeps dipping, you might have to prepare yourself for a reduction in its value. An increasing high might indicate a coming increase in the stock's worth.

Price-to-Earnings Ratio

Price-to-earnings ratio is also known as the P/E ratio. When you see this number next to a stock's stats, know that it is the company's share price compared to the earnings per share. To find the P/E ratio, you divide the share price by the earnings per share.

Investors use a price-to-earnings ratio to determine if a company's stock is undervalued or overvalued. If the P/E ratio is 50 or above, it is typically overvalued. If it is one or less, then it is considered undervalued. Seeing if a stock is undervalued or overvalued helps because you can decide if this company has room to grow or not. But keep in mind that those numbers do not always represent a companies long term value.

Open & Close

You probably already know the meaning of these words. But what does it mean in stock investing? Open is the price of the stock at the start of the day. Close is the price of the stock at the end of the day. So, you see that it is almost the same as what you already knew the words meant - open to start the day and close to end the day.

People look at the open and close for day trading and compare how the stock did that day. These figures are something to keep an eye on if you are day trading because it is essentially the two most important prices that stock hits on a trading day.

With the understanding of these terms, you are ready to start preparing for your foray into investing. Let's get you ready!

Chapter 4

Starting Your Investing Journey

In this chapter, I will focus on two big aspects of investing. One is making money as a teen to invest. The second is how much you need to invest as a first-time investor.

Your journey to becoming an expert investor making passive income without leaving your house starts now. I am here to show you all the ways it is possible. Let's start!

Making Money To Invest

Making money to invest as a teen might seem difficult because of the sometimes high price of a single share of stock. But when you look at the money-making options, it's not as difficult as it seems. You can save up enough to do your first investment trial.

You can get a job anywhere if you are 16 years old or older. It is relatively easy. But if you are younger, you might have to get creative. I have taken the liberty to explain some of the things you can do. So, no excuses for not making money to invest in your stock.

Neighborhood Jobs

One thing you can do is neighborhood jobs. Cutting grass, power washing driveways, raking leaves, or washing cars can help you raise money for your first stock. These tasks might seem minor and only fetch you a few dollars. But if you keep at it, you can start to earn more.

All you have to do is recognize a needed service in your neighborhood and start telling people you can do it for a particular price. Once you have gotten the market, the money will keep coming in steadily.

Household Chores

There are also options within your household. You can ask your parents if they can give you a job to get paid, even if it is a small amount of money at a time. It would be something aside from your regular chores, so it is clear that you are putting in extra effort to make money.

For example, jobs in the house could be washing your parents' cars, giving your mother a massage, shining your dad's shoes, taking out the trash, cleaning the fridge, etc. You can also do these chores for your older siblings and get paid by them. You might also get monetary gifts for family members. While you might not want to keep all of it, you should keep some of it to invest.

Sell Old Items

Another great sector to make money as a kid is selling old items. Do you have any old toys, books, stuffed animals, shoes, or clothes? If you say yes to any of these, there is no need to let them gather dust in the house. Use these to make some investing money. Ensure you seek your parent's permission before you sell anything off, though.

You can also ask your parents if they have anything old, they will not mind you selling it. Electronic devices you don't use anymore are an excellent selling option—things like a Nintendo DS, an old iPad, iPhone, Kindle, etc.

Where Can You Sell Your Old Items?

I will give you a list of some of the best and most popular platforms to sell your stuff and their pros and cons, so you don't have to go in unknowing.

Some of the best are:

- Facebook Marketplace
- eBay
- Craigslist

The first and biggest pro of Facebook Marketplace is that it is free to sell. All you need is a Facebook account. Next, it's easy to set up something to sell. You need to take pictures of it, describe the item you're selling, set a price, and you're good to go. Another pro is the audience. Almost every three out of four people in the U.S. have Facebook, so the reach is broad.

The final pro is communication. Since Facebook is a social media platform made to interact with others online, you can directly message potential customers via Facebook messenger about something you're selling on Facebook Marketplace.

The Facebook Marketplace's biggest con is safety. You can't know how legit the person selling the item is and if the sale goes through on both sides. But since you are the one who is selling, you can avoid getting scammed. Another con is Facebook Marketplace has a local pickup, which can be convenient and dangerous, so go over that with your parents before setting that up. You also have the option of shipping which is safe and what I recommend.

Next, we have eBay, which has been around for many years and is a household name in the online shopping world. For the pros, eBay has about 109 million users a month, so the audience is large. eBay also works like an auction, which is helpful because you can get more money for whatever you sell.

Another pro is that it's easy to set up being a seller. You only have to make an account if you do not already have one. For the cons, there are seller fees even if you sell nothing. There is also a lot of competition with other sellers and few options to promote your stuff within the platform.

Finally, we have Craigslist. With Craigslist, the biggest pro is that it is free to start with no monthly payments, like Facebook Marketplace. Unlike eBay, when you list something to be sold, it lasts 30 days for free, which is more than eBay's paid 10-day max listing with fees kept in mind.

The cons of Craigslist are that you have to be actively posting your item to be noticed by a buyer. There is also the fact that scammers are common on this platform, so be mindful of who you do business with. I recommend Facebook Marketplace because of the audience, no cost, and communication.

So, there are no excuses for not knowing how to make money to start investing just because you are a teenager. What you need to do is commit yourself to the process of making money. It will truly not be challenging but building a future for oneself is never a walk in the park. Starting now, you give yourself a head start on the future.

How Much Money Should You Invest?

That's the big question. The answer is not thousands of dollars. I'm sure most of you don't even have that much money. You only need a couple of hundred dollars or even one hundred dollars to invest.

Now it's better to invest more money because the more you invest, the more you make. But since we're not all millionaires, a hundred or two hundred plus works as a start, but preferably start with $600-1000 so you can get an even better start. There are some investment platforms where you can buy fractional shares, such as Robinhood (which I will get more into later).

Fractional shares essentially mean if a stock costs five hundred dollars but you don't have to have that much to invest in it, you can buy it for a fraction of the share. For example, when I'm writing this, Tesla's stock is $703. Now that's a lot of money for one share, but you can buy a dollar or more with fractional shares, so a percentage of the share is what you own.

This fractional buying helps because you can buy good and expensive stocks without paying the full price. Or, if you own a share and want to buy more but can't afford that, you could buy half of another share which is better than nothing. So, in terms of making money to invest, know you don't need too much to start.

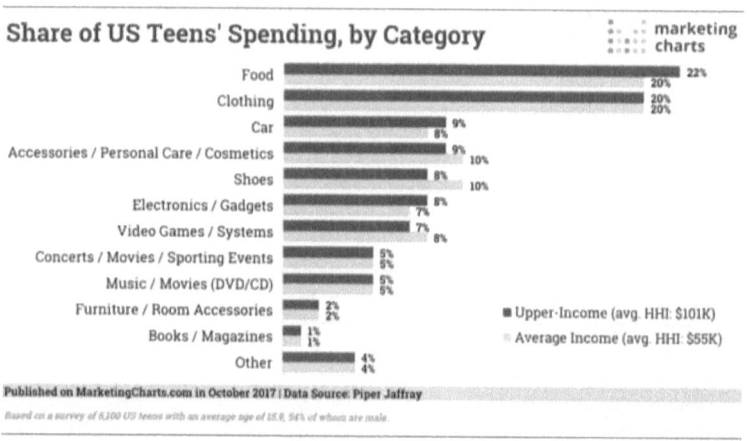

As this chart shows, there are many things you currently spend your money on and some of these things do not have the long term value that investment brings. Before you argue that these things are important, I am not saying that you shouldn't spend your money on them at all. I am saying you can cut back your expenses on these things to save for your investment.

I want to review just one of these top five things, food. Most people spend a good amount of their money on this, and I don't mean grocieries. However, the truth is that if you can cut back on it in certain ways, you might enjoy more money.

Let me break this down and explain how food does not have long-term value most of the time. And by the way, I am an avid food lover. However, you can cut back on the excess so you have money to put into your investing account. For example, you might buy fast food a few times a week, pick up a coffee before school or buy candy at a gas station.

That extra candy you buy will not add any value to your life in the long term. You can get more money to invest if you cut back on your excessive use of certain things. The fact that you can afford it doesn't mean you should buy it. Once you have learned to curb your appetite for things, you will have more money to invest in your portfolio.

Chapter 5

What To Look For In A Stock?

You can't just pick any company and buy its stock. That is a surefire way to lose your money. There are several factors you need to look for in a stock.

When looking at a stock to decide whether or not you will invest in it, you should first look at some key factors: the company's history, what the company plans to do, and the charts. These factors will help determine if the stock works for your goal - building wealth.

The Company's History

When looking into a company's history, there are a few things to research. One is who created it. The origin of the company and the reason for its creation are also important. Next, what does the company offer to its consumers? Check if the company has a reputation for excellently delivering whatever product or service they have. These questions help you figure out what the company is all about and what it stands for.

Why are these things important to know? Who created the company? That is important to know because the person that runs the company determines the success of the company. In other words, I would invest in someone's company if the CEO has a good track record, is known to be a good person, wants the best, and will do whatever it takes for that company to succeed.

That is why if I ask you to choose between the stocks of a company without an owner and the stocks of one of Elon Musk's companies, you will most likely pick the latter. You know the owner of the business as a good businessman, so it is easier for you to trust that the stocks of the company will do well over the years. Take time to understand the CEO of the company and their vision for the business.

With the origin of the company, look for why it was created, what problem it was seeking to solve, or what it was seeking to make better. That will also lead you to the reason for its creation and what the company offers. If it was created for something people will use forever, like Amazon or Apple, that's a good indicator to invest in that company.

Finally, with reputation, look into their reviews, articles, and blogs from customers. You can have the greatest idea in history, but if you can't provide it properly, then you're done.

The Company's Plans

Next, we dive into the company's plans for the future. You can look at articles online about what the company's CEO and leaders say about what's in store. Keep looking for promising innovations and updates when reading through articles and researching. If you see these features, that's a good indicator that the stock could be a good long-term buy. Any company that is not constantly growing and innovating will soon encounter problems as other companies leave them in the past. So, it is essential for the company to innovate and create new products to satisfy customers' demands.

For example, let's say Tesla announced they are releasing some new cars that everyone is excited about. When you hear that, a lightbulb should turn on in your head, saying that it's probably a good investment because of the prospect of more money for Tesla, meaning more money in their stock, meaning more money for you.

The Charts

Lastly, we have the charts. The charts can be found on any platform or online by searching the company's stock. They are a great factor to consider before investing in a stock because they show the most important information. It shows you how the stock has done over time. The charts I will be using as examples are from the stock Enphase Energy (ENPH).

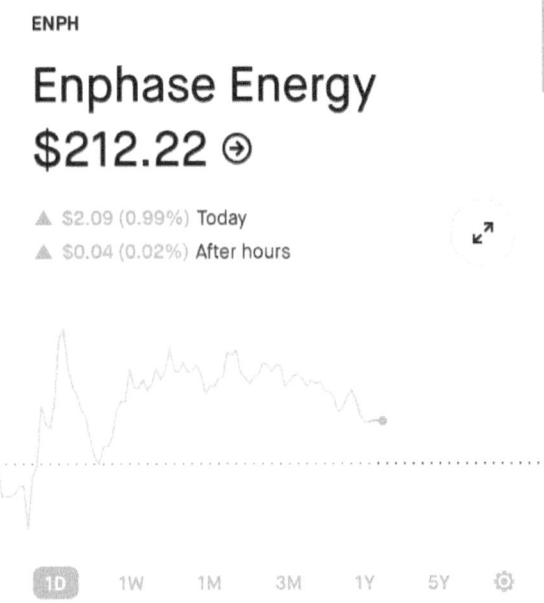

When you look at the chart for a stock, it tells you most of what you need to know about it, if it has grown or not. Because, ultimately, that is what you want as an investor. Every chart has significance, and I'll tell you what each means and its importance. With a 24-hour or one-day chart, you don't need to worry about it unless you're day trading. A stock's day-to-day ups and downs don't matter in the long run.

We also have the one-week or 5-day chart because the stock market is only open Monday through Friday, in case you didn't know. With this chart, it still doesn't matter that much in the long term, but it's good to check now and then to see how the market is doing in the short term. But all in all, don't worry about charts like the 24-hour one.

Next, we have the one-month chart. This one is more important to watch than the one-day has done. I'll put the one-year chart and five-year chart together.

ENPH

Enphase Energy
$212.22 ⊙

▲ $87.22 (69.78%) Past year

1D 1W 1M 3M **1Y** 5Y

ENPH

Enphase Energy
$212.22 ⊙

▲ $210.08 (9,816.82%) Past 5 years

1D 1W 1M 3M 1Y **5Y**

These charts are the ones you want to pay attention to the most because investing is not a short-term game. It takes years to decades to hold the stocks to get more money. So when researching a stock, check those charts because they show the long-term growth or decline of that company. If it has steadily gone upwards in price over these time frames, that is a good indicator to invest in it because that shows consistent growth.

Chapter 6

Best Investing Platforms For Beginners

Now you're ready to start, but what platform(s) should you invest in, especially for your first time? There is a multitude of great investing platforms that professionals use, but those can be complicated. More advanced platforms cost money anyways.

So, I picked two of the best investing platforms for beginners - Robinhood and Webull. Now we will go over the pros and cons of both.

Robinhood

Robinhood is a popular platform for investing, available as an app or on the web. It is commission free, meaning there are no payments to use it.

With Robinhood, you can invest in stocks, cryptocurrency, index funds, and ETFs. Their interface is user-friendly and simple to navigate. The platform is best made for mobile, as it is convenient to use on the go. It is easy to find, buy, and sell stocks.

They also have fractional shares, which means you don't have to buy a stock at the full price. Instead, you can buy it for a fraction of that share, and that feature is especially nice when you want to buy good stocks that cost a lot of money. Another great thing they offer is a Roth IRA account, which is a retirement account that you can put up to six thousand dollars a year into, and it is tax free when you take it out at the age of 59.

One major con of Robinhood is that their customer service isn't the best, from personal experience. They don't have a number to call if you have a question.

Instead, they have a message system that most people, including myself, find unreliable.

Webull

Webull, like Robinhood, is also commission free. With them, you can invest in stocks, cryptocurrency, and ETFs. They also offer fractional shares similar to Robinhood. Unlike Robinhood, Webull has a number to call for any help you might need, but some have said that it is not that reliable.

Another thing they have is more advanced analytics which is excellent for research. However, Webull's interface is a little more confusing than Robinhood's because of all the charts and data they have. It can be overwhelming for a first-time investor. But the information is helpful, and their charts are better than Robinhood.

Let me summarize my thoughts about both platforms and say which one I think is best for beginning investors. Webull is great for first-time investors because it is free, and they have a lot of good data on stocks. Also, compared to most brokerages besides

Robinhood, Webull is not difficult to navigate. Robinhood is easy to use and offers much, such as fractional shares and a Roth IRA account.

On the other hand, Webull can be overwhelming for first-time investors because of more complex charts and more data overall compared to Robinhood. So, in conclusion, the platform I would recommend is Robinhood because of how simple it is to navigate and the ease of use on mobile devices.

You might ask if it is okay to use both platforms or more than one platform in general. I would say yes because every stock platform has good and bad things, and using more than one platform can even things out. So, for example, if you want to invest in cryptocurrency but are worried that it might mess up your stock investments, I'd advise you to use two platforms so whatever you invest in has its full chance to flourish.

Chapter 7

The Mental Game

This chapter will cover one of the most difficult parts of investing - the mental part. Many poor investment decisions are made based on emotions such as fear and greed. Some of these decisions are based on other people via articles, YouTube, Reddit, Twitter, etc. Many of these decisions end up turning sour, and you lose money.

So, I will explain how to not give in to emotion and mess up your investment. You should also know when and why you should tune out the internet.

Do Not Fear

The first emotion I will discuss is fear. This emotion is something that almost every investor has experienced when the market goes down, either by a small amount or a large amount. This situation causes fear because you are watching your stocks decrease in value and losing money.

Most people sell their stock because they do not want to lose any more money. Which makes sense, right? NO! Think of it like this: stocks are cheaper when the market drops. When you see a dip in the market, that should be an indicator to buy more, especially when the stock is good.

Then when the market goes up, you make more money because you bought in for cheaper. So, remember that when the market goes down, and your stocks lose value, do not give in to fear and sell everything.

Instead, see it as an opportunity to make more money. Also, remember you will be starting way earlier than most investors, so time is on your side. So, do not be concerned about the short-term ups and downs of the market.

Do Not Be Greedy

The next emotion is greed. Greed has messed up my investments l several times. But from those mistakes, I learned contentment. You'll typically experience greed with investing while making money in a short-term trade like a day trade (where you buy and sell a stock on the same day to secure a quick profit).

What usually happens is you make money on a trade, then you want more, so you hold on to the trade instead of selling to secure your profit. However, the stock goes down, causing you to lose the money you already made and any chances of making more. So, the trick with greed is to be content you made money and sell it before it goes down.

Listen to the Right People

One of the most detrimental ways to lose money is doing what other people say you should do. So, the thing with investing is that it is good to take advice from someone professional, like a financial advisor or someone respected among the investment community, like Warren Buffet or a top-notch YouTuber, such as those I have mentioned earlier in this book.

On the flip side, many people share their thoughts on what you should invest in. These people make it sound like they know what they are talking about. Some do, but generally, they lead you astray. So, when you see someone post what they are investing in or trading in and say they made a lot of money from it, do not blindly follow them and copy their investment.

Stick to the investment plan you had already but if you are curious, do thorough research on what they said they did and that person to see if they are legitimate. I have had to turn my ears away from most of the news about investing. You will have to do the same. But there are still reliable people on these platforms. Take YouTube, for instance. It is full of people I am subscribed to who are well-known, well-respected, and have a track record of success. You will have to learn how to filter what is good from the numerous pieces of content you will find on several media pages. Don't follow any source that has proven to give unreliable advice or induce fear. Ultimately, the things you see and hear about investing determine the trajectory of your outcome.

Understand that making loads of money in the stock market does not happen in a few days, months, or years. So, please be patient and trust the process because when you have a ton of money from no physical labor, no nine to five, you will thank your younger self for deciding to start now.

Conclusion

Only knowledge applied to your life benefits you!

I am truly grateful that you have taken the time to read this book up to this point and that you have learned all the basics of stock investing as a teenager. However, the entire purpose of reading this book will be defeated if you don't start working on becoming an investing teenager.

As I have explained, the process can be easy. However, it will take grit and determination to follow through to the end and make yourself an admirable investing teenager. But don't be discouraged. All you have to do is take the first step, and it will be easier to take the next one.

For some of you, it will be starting to save up money for your stock investment. For some, you already have money saved up. So, you can start familiarizing yourself with the best investing platforms for beginners that I mentioned. Whatever the first step that you have to take to start investing, don't delay it. Don't procrastinate.

Once you have started your journey, you might face different challenges. You will be tempted to give up several times. I was also tempted and wanted to stop the entire process. But no matter the loss or pain, if you continue investing, the wins will outweigh the losses in the end.

Start building wealth for your future. You are not too young to start making smart financial decisions. You can do it!

Your future self will thank you for taking that first step today.

Four Steps:

1. Save up $100-$1000
2. Open an account with your parents.
3. Research companies to invest in thoroughly. (Or just invest in index funds, ETFs, or blue chip stocks like Apple, Microsoft, and Tesla.)
4. Now you're ready to make your very first investment. Remember to be patient, and enjoy the process!

www.ingramcontent.com/pod-product-compliance
Lightning Source LLC
Chambersburg PA
CBHW030459220526
45464CB00006B/2586